Contents

Foreword

The National Curriculum lies at the heart of our policies to raise standards. It sets out a clear, full and statutory entitlement to learning for all pupils. It determines the content of what will be taught, and sets attainment targets for learning. It also determines how performance will be assessed and reported. An effective National Curriculum therefore gives teachers, pupils, parents, employers and their wider community a clear and shared understanding of the skills and knowledge that young people will gain at school. It allows schools to meet the individual learning needs of pupils and to develop a distinctive character and ethos rooted in their local communities. And it provides a framework within which all partners in education can support young people on the road to further learning.

Getting the National Curriculum right presents difficult choices and balances. It must be robust enough to define and defend the core of knowledge and cultural experience which is the entitlement of every pupil, and at the same time flexible enough to give teachers the scope to build their teaching around it in ways which will enhance its delivery to their pupils.

The focus of this National Curriculum, together with the wider school curriculum, is therefore to ensure that pupils develop from an early age the essential literacy and numeracy skills they need to learn; to provide them with a guaranteed, full and rounded entitlement to learning; to foster their creativity; and to give teachers discretion to find the best ways to inspire in their pupils a joy and commitment to learning that will last a lifetime.

An entitlement to learning must be an entitlement for all pupils. This National Curriculum includes for the first time a detailed, overarching statement on inclusion which makes clear the principles schools must follow in their teaching right across the curriculum, to ensure that all pupils have the chance to succeed, whatever their individual needs and the potential barriers to their learning may be.

Equality of opportunity is one of a broad set of common values and purposes which underpin the school curriculum and the work of schools. These also include a commitment to valuing ourselves, our families and other relationships, the wider groups to which we belong, the diversity in our society and the environment in which we live. Until now, ours was one of the few national curricula not to have a statement of rationale setting out the fundamental principles underlying the curriculum. The handbooks for primary and secondary teachers include for the first time such a statement.

This is also the first National Curriculum in England to include citizenship, from September 2002, as part of the statutory curriculum for secondary schools. Education in citizenship and democracy will provide coherence in the way in which all pupils are helped to develop a full understanding of their roles and responsibilities as citizens in a modern democracy. It will play an important role, alongside other aspects of the curriculum and school life, in helping pupils to deal with difficult moral and social questions that arise in their lives and in society. The handbooks also provide for the first time a national framework for the teaching of personal, social and health education. Both elements reflect the fact that education is also about helping pupils to develop the knowledge, skills and understanding they need to live confident, healthy, independent lives, as individuals, parents, workers and members of society.

Rt Hon David Blunkett
Secretary of State for Education and Employment

Sir William Stubbs
Chairman, Qualifications and Curriculum Authority

About this booklet

This booklet:

- sets out the legal requirements of the National Curriculum in England for modern foreign languages (MFL)
- provides information to help teachers implement modern foreign languages in their schools.

It has been written for coordinators, subject leaders and those who teach MFL, and is one of a series of separate booklets for each National Curriculum subject.

The National Curriculum for pupils aged five to 11 is set out in the handbook for primary teachers. The National Curriculum for pupils aged 11 to 16 is set out in the handbook for secondary teachers.

All these publications, and materials that support the teaching, learning and assessment of MFL, can be found on the National Curriculum web site at www.nc.uk.net.

About modern foreign languages in the National Curriculum

The structure of the National Curriculum

The programme of study[1] sets out what pupils should be taught, and the attainment targets set out the expected standards of pupils' performance. It is for schools to choose how they organise their school curriculum to include the programme of study for modern foreign languages (MFL).

The programme of study

The programme of study sets out what pupils should be taught in MFL at key stages 3 and 4 and provides the basis for planning schemes of work. When planning, schools should also consider the general teaching requirements for inclusion, use of language and use of information and communication technology that apply across the programme of study.

The **Knowledge, skills and understanding** in the programme of study identify the aspects of MFL in which pupils make progress:

- acquiring knowledge and understanding of the target language
- developing language skills
- developing language-learning skills
- developing cultural awareness.

These aspects of modern foreign languages are developed through communicating in the target language in a range of contexts and for a variety of purposes, as set out in **Breadth of study**.

Schools may find the DfEE/QCA exemplar schemes of work helpful to show how the programme of study and attainment targets can be translated into practical, manageable teaching plans.

Guidelines for the teaching of MFL at key stage 2 are included in this booklet. They are designed to promote the teaching of MFL in primary schools and improve progression to secondary schools.

[1] The Education Act 1996, section 353b, defines a programme of study as the 'matters, skills and processes' that should be taught to pupils of different abilities and maturities during the key stage.

Attainment targets and level descriptions

The attainment targets for MFL set out the 'knowledge, skills and understanding that pupils of different abilities and maturities are expected to have by the end of each key stage'[2]. Attainment targets consist of eight level descriptions of increasing difficulty, plus a description for exceptional performance above level 8. Each level description describes the types and range of performance that pupils working at that level should characteristically demonstrate.

In MFL, there are four attainment targets that are organised under the four language skills of listening, speaking, reading and writing. Activities will often cover two or more of these language skills.

While the level descriptions for MFL indicate progression in the knowledge, skills and understanding set out in the programme of study, they do not refer specifically to any topic or aspect of grammar. This is because the level descriptions apply to a wide range of different languages, each with its distinctive features. There are specific modifications for Chinese and Japanese. For languages with non-Roman scripts, the level descriptions assume pre-reading skills (recognising letters/syllables, printed/handwritten forms) and pre-writing skills (forming letters, joining letters, making strokes in the correct order).

The level descriptions provide the basis on which to make judgements about pupils' performance at the end of key stage 3. At key stage 4, national qualifications are the main means of assessing attainment in MFL.

Although MFL is not a statutory subject until key stage 3, the level descriptions for MFL are designed to enable the majority of pupils to make progress more rapidly through the lower levels. The expectation at the end of key stage 3 is therefore the same as for all other subjects.

Range of levels within which the great majority of pupils are expected to work		Expected attainment for the majority of pupils at the end of the key stage	
Key stage 3	**3–7**	at age 14	**5/6**

Assessing attainment at the end of key stage 3

In deciding on a pupil's level of attainment at the end of key stage 3, teachers should judge which description best fits the pupil's performance. When doing so, each description should be considered alongside descriptions for adjacent levels.

Arrangements for statutory assessment at the end of each key stage are set out in detail in QCA's annual booklets about assessment and reporting arrangements.

[2] As defined by the Education Act 1996, section 353a.

Learning across the National Curriculum

The importance of MFL to pupils' education is set out on page 14. The handbooks for primary and secondary teachers also set out in general terms how the National Curriculum can promote learning across the curriculum in a number of areas such as spiritual, moral, social and cultural development, key skills and thinking skills. The examples below indicate specific ways in which the teaching of MFL can contribute to learning across the curriculum.

Promoting pupils' spiritual, moral, social and cultural development through MFL

For example, MFL provides opportunities to promote:

- *spiritual development,* through stimulating pupils' interest and fascination in the phenomenon of language and the meanings and feelings it can transmit
- *moral development,* through helping pupils formulate and express opinions in the target language about issues of right and wrong
- *social development,* through exploring different social conventions, such as forms of address, through developing pupils' ability to communicate with others, particularly speakers of foreign languages, in an appropriate, sympathetic and tolerant manner, and through fostering the spirit of cooperation when using a foreign language to communicate with other people, whether other learners or native speakers
- *cultural development,* through providing pupils with insights into cultural differences and opportunities to relate these to their own experience and to consider different cultural and linguistic traditions, attitudes and behaviours.

Promoting key skills through MFL

For example, MFL provides opportunities for pupils to develop the key skills of:

- *communication,* through developing their awareness of the way language is structured and how it can be manipulated to meet a range of needs, and through reinforcing learning in specific areas such as listening, reading for gist and detail, and using grammar correctly
- *application of number,* through talking and writing about the time and measures in the target language, and carrying out conversions about distances and currency
- *IT,* through using audio, video, satellite television and the internet to access and communicate information, and through selecting and using a range of ICT resources to create presentations for different audiences and purposes
- *working with others,* through developing their ability to participate in group conversations and discussions
- *improving own learning and performance,* through developing their ability to rehearse and redraft work to improve accuracy and presentation, and through developing learning strategies such as memorising, dealing with the unpredictable, and using reference materials
- *problem solving,* through developing their ability to apply and adapt their knowledge of the target language for specific communication purposes.

Promoting other aspects of the curriculum

For example, MFL provides opportunities to promote:

- *thinking skills,* through developing pupils' ability to draw inferences from unfamiliar language and unexpected responses, through enabling pupils to reflect on the links between languages, and through developing pupils' creative use of language and expression of their own ideas, attitudes and opinions
- *financial capability,* through knowledge of different currencies and exchange rates
- *work-related learning,* through opportunities to cover work-related contexts within the topic of the world of work.

The programme of study for modern foreign languages

A common structure and design for all subjects

The programmes of study

The National Curriculum programmes of study have been given a common structure and a common design.

In each subject, at each key stage, the main column **1** contains the programme of study, which sets out two sorts of requirements:

- **Knowledge, skills and understanding** **2** – what has to be taught in the subject during the key stage
- **Breadth of study** **3** – the contexts, activities, areas of study and range of experiences through which the **Knowledge, skills and understanding** should be taught.

Schools are not required by law to teach the content in grey type. This includes the examples in the main column **4** [printed inside square brackets], all text in the margins **5** and information and examples in the inclusion statement.

The programmes of study for English, mathematics and science

The programmes of study for English and science contain sections that correspond directly to the attainment targets for each subject. In mathematics this one-to-one correspondence does not hold for all key stages – see the mathematics programme of study for more information. In English, the three sections of the programme of study each contain **Breadth of study** requirements. In mathematics and science there is a single, separate set of **Breadth of study** requirements for each key stage.

The programmes of study in the non-core foundation subjects

In these subjects (except for citizenship) the programme of study simply contains two sets of requirements – **Knowledge, skills and understanding** and **Breadth of study**. The programmes of study for citizenship contain no **Breadth of study** requirements.

Information in the margins

At the start of each key stage, the margin begins with a summary **6** of the main things that pupils will learn during the key stage. The margins also contain four other types of non-statutory information:

- notes giving key information that should be taken into account when teaching the subject
- notes giving definitions of words and phrases in the programmes of study
- suggested opportunities for pupils to use information and communication technology (ICT) as they learn the subject
- some key links with other subjects indicating connections between teaching requirements, and suggesting how a requirement in one subject can build on the requirements in another in the same key stage.

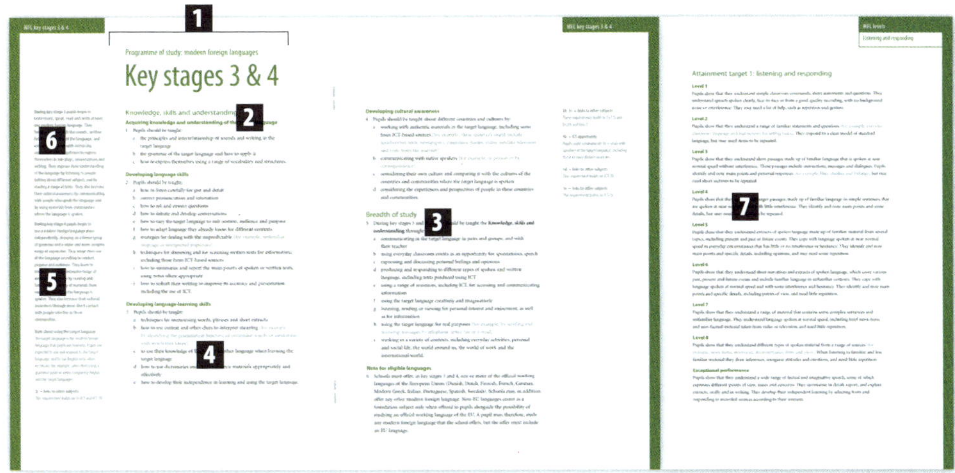

The referencing system

References work as follows:

A reference in …	… reads …	… and means …
Physical education key stage 2	11a, 11b → links to other subjects These requirements build on Gg/2c.	Physical education key stage 2, requirements 11a and 11b build on geography (key stage 2), paragraph 2, requirement c.
Art and design key stage 1	4a → links to other subjects This requirement builds on Ma3/2a, 2c, 2d.	Art and design key stage 1, requirement 4a builds on mathematics (key stage 1), Ma3 Shape, space and measures, paragraph 2, requirements a, c and d.
Citizenship key stage 3	1a → links to other subjects This requirement builds on Hi/10, 13.	Citizenship key stage 3, requirement 1a builds on history (key stage 3) paragraphs 10 and 13.

The attainment targets

The attainment targets **7** are at the end of this booklet. They can be read alongside the programmes of study by folding out the flaps.

The importance of modern foreign languages

Through the study of a foreign language, pupils understand and appreciate different countries, cultures, people and communities – and as they do so, begin to think of themselves as citizens of the world as well as of the United Kingdom. Pupils also learn about the basic structures of language. They explore the similarities and differences between the foreign language they are learning and English or another language, and learn how language can be manipulated and applied in different ways. Their listening, reading and memory skills improve, and their speaking and writing become more accurate. The development of these skills, together with pupils' knowledge and understanding of the structure of language, lay the foundations for future study of other languages.

Ich bin umweltfreundlich und ich verwende umweltfreundliche Produkte. Ich finde Umweltschutz sehr wichtig also kaufe ich keine Spraydosen. Jede Woche bringe ich meine Glasflaschen zu dem Altglascontainer am supermarkt und ich recycle mein Papier und Plastik.

My wife and I learnt Spanish and Japanese when I played at Barcelona and Nagoya. We spent hours and hours in tuition – yet we could have learnt either language years earlier at school. Modern languages prepare you for modern life.

Gary Lineker, Footballer and Television Presenter

Learning a language makes our minds stronger and more flexible. Actually using it gives us an entirely new experience of the world.

John Cleese, Actor

Learning another language is part of making the civilised world go around, so start early.

Sir Peter Parker, Chair, DTI National Languages for Export Campaign

It is arrogant to assume that we can get by in English or that everyone else will speak our language. Learning a foreign language is polite, demonstrates commitment – and in today's world is absolutely necessary.

Sir Trevor McDonald, Chair, Nuffield Languages Inquiry

Pourquoi étudier les langues?

A mon avis c'est très important d'étudier les langues et je pense que tout le monde devrait le faire.

Les langues permettent de voyager à l'étranger sans avoir de difficultés de communication. Si on sait parler la langue du pays, les vacances sont plus amusantes. On peut faire de nouvelles connaissances, rencontrer des amis et généralement c'est plus facile d'obtenir des informations. C'est essentiel pour encourager de bonnes relations internationales, surtout de nos jours quand il y a beaucoup de conflits.

Es muy importante aprender porque al colegio venimos a ser inteligentes, listos e ingeniosos, así que nosotros no somos tontos.

Programme of study: modern foreign languages

Key stages 3 & 4

During key stage 3 pupils begin to understand, speak, read and write at least one modern foreign language. They become familiar with the sounds, written form and grammar of the language, and use this knowledge with increasing confidence and competence to express themselves in role plays, conversations and writing. They improve their understanding of the language by listening to people talking about different subjects and by reading a range of texts. They also increase their cultural awareness by communicating with people who speak the language and by using materials from countries and communities where the language is spoken.

During key stage 4 pupils begin to use a modern foreign language more independently, drawing on a firmer grasp of grammar and a wider and more complex range of expression. They adapt their use of the language according to context, purpose and audience. They learn to understand a more extensive range of unfamiliar language by reading and listening to a variety of materials from countries and communities where the language is spoken. They also increase their cultural awareness through more direct contact with people who live in those countries and communities.

Note about using the target language

The target language is the modern foreign language that pupils are learning. Pupils are expected to use and respond to the target language, and to use English only when necessary (for example, when discussing a grammar point or when comparing English and the target language).

Knowledge, skills and understanding

Acquiring knowledge and understanding of the target language

1 Pupils should be taught:

- a the principles and interrelationship of sounds and writing in the target language
- b the grammar of the target language and how to apply it
- c how to express themselves using a range of vocabulary and structures.

Developing language skills

2 Pupils should be taught:

- a how to listen carefully for gist and detail
- b correct pronunciation and intonation
- c how to ask and answer questions
- d how to initiate and develop conversations
- e how to vary the target language to suit context, audience and purpose
- f how to adapt language they already know for different contexts
- g strategies for dealing with the unpredictable [for example, unfamiliar language, unexpected responses]
- h techniques for skimming and for scanning written texts for information, including those from ICT-based sources
- i how to summarise and report the main points of spoken or written texts, using notes where appropriate
- j how to redraft their writing to improve its accuracy and presentation, including the use of ICT.

Developing language-learning skills

3 Pupils should be taught:

- a techniques for memorising words, phrases and short extracts
- b how to use context and other clues to interpret meaning [for example, by identifying the grammatical function of unfamiliar words or similarities with words they know]
- c to use their knowledge of English or another language when learning the target language
- d how to use dictionaries and other reference materials appropriately and effectively
- e how to develop their independence in learning and using the target language.

Developing cultural awareness

4 Pupils should be taught about different countries and cultures by:

a working with authentic materials in the target language, including some from ICT-based sources [for example, handwritten texts, newspapers, magazines, books, video, satellite television, texts from the internet]

b communicating with native speakers [for example, in person, by correspondence]

c considering their own culture and comparing it with the cultures of the countries and communities where the target language is spoken

d considering the experiences and perspectives of people in these countries and communities.

Breadth of study

5 During key stages 3 and 4, pupils should be taught the **Knowledge, skills and understanding** through:

a communicating in the target language in pairs and groups, and with their teacher

b using everyday classroom events as an opportunity for spontaneous speech

c expressing and discussing personal feelings and opinions

d producing and responding to different types of spoken and written language, including texts produced using ICT

e using a range of resources, including ICT, for accessing and communicating information

f using the target language creatively and imaginatively

g listening, reading or viewing for personal interest and enjoyment, as well as for information

h using the target language for real purposes [for example, by sending and receiving messages by telephone, letter, fax or e-mail]

i working in a variety of contexts, including everyday activities, personal and social life, the world around us, the world of work and the international world.

Note for eligible languages

6 Schools must offer, in key stages 3 and 4, one or more of the official working languages of the European Union (Danish, Dutch, Finnish, French, German, Modern Greek, Italian, Portuguese, Spanish, Swedish). Schools may, in addition, offer any other modern foreign language. Non-EU languages count as a foundation subject only when offered to pupils alongside the possibility of studying an official working language of the EU. A pupil may, therefore, study any modern foreign language that the school offers, but the offer must include an EU language.

1b, 3c → links to other subjects
These requirements build on En1/5 and En2/6 and En3/7.

2j → links to other subjects
This requirement builds on En3/2 and ICT/3b.

4b → ICT opportunity
Pupils could communicate by e-mail with speakers of the target language, including those in more distant countries.

5d → links to other subjects
This requirement builds on ICT/3b.

5e → links to other subjects
This requirement builds on ICT/3c.

General teaching requirements

Inclusion: providing effective learning opportunities for all pupils

Schools have a responsibility to provide a broad and balanced curriculum for all pupils. The National Curriculum is the starting point for planning a school curriculum that meets the specific needs of individuals and groups of pupils. This statutory inclusion statement on providing effective learning opportunities for all pupils outlines how teachers can modify, as necessary, the National Curriculum programmes of study to provide all pupils with relevant and appropriately challenging work at each key stage. It sets out three principles that are essential to developing a more inclusive curriculum:

A Setting suitable learning challenges
B Responding to pupils' diverse learning needs
C Overcoming potential barriers to learning and assessment for individuals and groups of pupils.

Applying these principles should keep to a minimum the need for aspects of the National Curriculum to be disapplied for a pupil.

Schools are able to provide other curricular opportunities outside the National Curriculum to meet the needs of individuals or groups of pupils such as speech and language therapy and mobility training.

Three principles for inclusion

In planning and teaching the National Curriculum, teachers are required to have due regard to the following principles.

A Setting suitable learning challenges

1 Teachers should aim to give every pupil the opportunity to experience success in learning and to achieve as high a standard as possible. The National Curriculum programmes of study set out what most pupils should be taught at each key stage – but teachers should teach the knowledge, skills and understanding in ways that suit their pupils' abilities. This may mean choosing knowledge, skills and understanding from earlier or later key stages so that individual pupils can make progress and show what they can achieve. Where it is appropriate for pupils to make extensive use of content from an earlier key stage, there may not be time to teach all aspects of the age-related programmes of study. A similarly flexible approach will be needed to take account of any gaps in pupils' learning resulting from missed or interrupted schooling [for example, that may be experienced by travellers, refugees, those in care or those with long-term medical conditions, including pupils with neurological problems, such as head injuries, and those with degenerative conditions]

2 For pupils whose attainments fall significantly below the expected levels at a particular key stage, a much greater degree of differentiation will be necessary. In these circumstances, teachers may need to use the content of the programmes of study as a resource or to provide a context, in planning learning appropriate to the age and requirements of their pupils.[1]

3 For pupils whose attainments significantly exceed the expected level of attainment within one or more subjects during a particular key stage, teachers will need to plan suitably challenging work. As well as drawing on materials from later key stages or higher levels of study, teachers may plan further differentiation by extending the breadth and depth of study within individual subjects or by planning work which draws on the content of different subjects.[2]

B Responding to pupils' diverse learning needs

1 When planning, teachers should set high expectations and provide opportunities for all pupils to achieve, including boys and girls, pupils with special educational needs, pupils with disabilities, pupils from all social and cultural backgrounds, pupils of different ethnic groups including travellers, refugees and asylum seekers, and those from diverse linguistic backgrounds. Teachers need to be aware that pupils bring to school different experiences, interests and strengths which will influence the way in which they learn. Teachers should plan their approaches to teaching and learning so that all pupils can take part in lessons fully and effectively.

2 To ensure that they meet the full range of pupils' needs, teachers should be aware of the requirements of the equal opportunities legislation that covers race, gender and disability.[3]

3 Teachers should take specific action to respond to pupils' diverse needs by:

- a creating effective learning environments
- b securing their motivation and concentration
- c providing equality of opportunity through teaching approaches
- d using appropriate assessment approaches
- e setting targets for learning.

Examples for B/3a – creating effective learning environments

Teachers create effective learning environments in which:

- the contribution of all pupils is valued
- all pupils can feel secure and are able to contribute appropriately
- stereotypical views are challenged and pupils learn to appreciate and view positively differences in others, whether arising from race, gender, ability or disability

[1] Teachers may find QCA's guidance on planning work for pupils with learning difficulties a helpful companion to the programmes of study.
[2] Teachers may find QCA's guidance on meeting the requirements of gifted and talented pupils a helpful companion to the programmes of study.
[3] The Sex Discrimination Act 1975, the Race Relations Act 1976, the Disability Discrimination Act 1995.

- pupils learn to take responsibility for their actions and behaviours both in school and in the wider community
- all forms of bullying and harassment, including racial harassment, are challenged
- pupils are enabled to participate safely in clothing appropriate to their religious beliefs, particularly in subjects such as science, design and technology and physical education.

Examples for B/3b – securing motivation and concentration

Teachers secure pupils' motivation and concentration by:

- using teaching approaches appropriate to different learning styles
- using, where appropriate, a range of organisational approaches, such as setting, grouping or individual work, to ensure that learning needs are properly addressed
- varying subject content and presentation so that this matches their learning needs
- planning work which builds on their interests and cultural experiences
- planning appropriately challenging work for those whose ability and understanding are in advance of their language skills
- using materials which reflect social and cultural diversity and provide positive images of race, gender and disability
- planning and monitoring the pace of work so that they all have a chance to learn effectively and achieve success
- taking action to maintain interest and continuity of learning for pupils who may be absent for extended periods of time.

Examples for B/3c – providing equality of opportunity

Teaching approaches that provide equality of opportunity include:

- ensuring that boys and girls are able to participate in the same curriculum, particularly in science, design and technology and physical education
- taking account of the interests and concerns of boys and girls by using a range of activities and contexts for work and allowing a variety of interpretations and outcomes, particularly in English, science, design and technology, ICT, art and design, music and physical education
- avoiding gender stereotyping when organising pupils into groups, assigning them to activities or arranging access to equipment, particularly in science, design and technology, ICT, music and physical education
- taking account of pupils' specific religious or cultural beliefs relating to the representation of ideas or experiences or to the use of particular types of equipment, particularly in science, design and technology, ICT and art and design
- enabling the fullest possible participation of pupils with disabilities or particular medical needs in all subjects, offering positive role models and making provision, where necessary, to facilitate access to activities with appropriate support, aids or adaptations. (See **Overcoming potential barriers to learning and assessment for individuals and groups of pupils.**)

Examples for B/3d – using appropriate assessment approaches

Teachers use appropriate assessment approaches that:

- allow for different learning styles and ensure that pupils are given the chance and encouragement to demonstrate their competence and attainment through appropriate means
- are familiar to the pupils and for which they have been adequately prepared
- use materials which are free from discrimination and stereotyping in any form
- provide clear and unambiguous feedback to pupils to aid further learning.

Examples for B/3e – setting targets for learning

Teachers set targets for learning that:

- build on pupils' knowledge, experiences, interests and strengths to improve areas of weakness and demonstrate progression over time
- are attainable and yet challenging and help pupils to develop their self-esteem and confidence in their ability to learn.

C Overcoming potential barriers to learning and assessment for individuals and groups of pupils

A minority of pupils will have particular learning and assessment requirements which go beyond the provisions described in sections A and B and, if not addressed, could create barriers to learning. These requirements are likely to arise as a consequence of a pupil having a special educational need or disability or may be linked to a pupil's progress in learning English as an additional language.

1 Teachers must take account of these requirements and make provision, where necessary, to support individuals or groups of pupils to enable them to participate effectively in the curriculum and assessment activities. During end of key stage assessments, teachers should bear in mind that special arrangements are available to support individual pupils.

Pupils with special educational needs

2 Curriculum planning and assessment for pupils with special educational needs must take account of the type and extent of the difficulty experienced by the pupil. Teachers will encounter a wide range of pupils with special educational needs, some of whom will also have disabilities (see paragraphs C/4 and C/5). In many cases, the action necessary to respond to an individual's requirements for curriculum access will be met through greater differentiation of tasks and materials, consistent with school-based intervention as set out in the SEN Code of Practice. A smaller number of pupils may need access to specialist equipment and approaches or to alternative or adapted activities, consistent with school-based intervention augmented by advice and support from external specialists as described in the SEN Code of Practice, or, in exceptional circumstances, with a statement of special educational need.

Teachers should, where appropriate, work closely with representatives of other agencies who may be supporting the pupil.

3 Teachers should take specific action to provide access to learning for pupils with special educational needs by:
- a providing for pupils who need help with communication, language and literacy
- b planning, where necessary, to develop pupils' understanding through the use of all available senses and experiences
- c planning for pupils' full participation in learning and in physical and practical activities
- d helping pupils to manage their behaviour, to take part in learning effectively and safely, and, at key stage 4, to prepare for work
- e helping individuals to manage their emotions, particularly trauma or stress, and to take part in learning.

Examples for C/3a – helping with communication, language and literacy
Teachers provide for pupils who need help with communication, language and literacy through:
- using texts that pupils can read and understand
- using visual and written materials in different formats, including large print, symbol text and Braille
- using ICT, other technological aids and taped materials
- using alternative and augmentative communication, including signs and symbols
- using translators, communicators and amanuenses.

Examples for C/3b – developing understanding
Teachers develop pupils' understanding through the use of all available senses and experiences, by:
- using materials and resources that pupils can access through sight, touch, sound, taste or smell
- using word descriptions and other stimuli to make up for a lack of first-hand experiences
- using ICT, visual and other materials to increase pupils' knowledge of the wider world
- encouraging pupils to take part in everyday activities such as play, drama, class visits and exploring the environment.

Examples for C/3c – planning for full participation
Teachers plan for pupils' full participation in learning and in physical and practical activities through:
- using specialist aids and equipment
- providing support from adults or peers when needed
- adapting tasks or environments
- providing alternative activities, where necessary.

Examples for C/3d – managing behaviour

Teachers help pupils to manage their behaviour, take part in learning effectively and safely, and, at key stage 4, prepare for work by:

- setting realistic demands and stating them explicitly
- using positive behaviour management, including a clear structure of rewards and sanctions
- giving pupils every chance and encouragement to develop the skills they need to work well with a partner or a group
- teaching pupils to value and respect the contribution of others
- encouraging and teaching independent working skills
- teaching essential safety rules.

Examples for C/3e – managing emotions

Teachers help individuals manage their emotions and take part in learning through:

- identifying aspects of learning in which the pupil will engage and plan short-term, easily achievable goals in selected activities
- providing positive feedback to reinforce and encourage learning and build self-esteem
- selecting tasks and materials sensitively to avoid unnecessary stress for the pupil
- creating a supportive learning environment in which the pupil feels safe and is able to engage with learning
- allowing time for the pupil to engage with learning and gradually increasing the range of activities and demands.

Pupils with disabilities

4 Not all pupils with disabilities will necessarily have special educational needs. Many pupils with disabilities learn alongside their peers with little need for additional resources beyond the aids which they use as part of their daily life, such as a wheelchair, a hearing aid or equipment to aid vision. Teachers must take action, however, in their planning to ensure that these pupils are enabled to participate as fully and effectively as possible within the National Curriculum and the statutory assessment arrangements. Potential areas of difficulty should be identified and addressed at the outset of work, without recourse to the formal provisions for disapplication.

5 Teachers should take specific action to enable the effective participation of pupils with disabilities by:

a planning appropriate amounts of time to allow for the satisfactory completion of tasks

b planning opportunities, where necessary, for the development of skills in practical aspects of the curriculum

c identifying aspects of programmes of study and attainment targets that may present specific difficulties for individuals.

Examples for C/5a – planning to complete tasks

Teachers plan appropriate amounts of time to allow pupils to complete tasks satisfactorily through:

- taking account of the very slow pace at which some pupils will be able to record work, either manually or with specialist equipment, and of the physical effort required
- being aware of the high levels of concentration necessary for some pupils when following or interpreting text or graphics, particularly when using vision aids or tactile methods, and of the tiredness which may result
- allocating sufficient time, opportunity and access to equipment for pupils to gain information through experimental work and detailed observation, including the use of microscopes
- being aware of the effort required by some pupils to follow oral work, whether through use of residual hearing, lip reading or a signer, and of the tiredness or loss of concentration which may occur.

Examples for C/5b – developing skills in practical aspects

Teachers create opportunities for the development of skills in practical aspects of the curriculum through:

- providing adapted, modified or alternative activities or approaches to learning in physical education and ensuring that these have integrity and equivalence to the National Curriculum and enable pupils to make appropriate progress
- providing alternative or adapted activities in science, art and design and design and technology for pupils who are unable to manipulate tools, equipment or materials or who may be allergic to certain types of materials
- ensuring that all pupils can be included and participate safely in geography fieldwork, local studies and visits to museums, historic buildings and sites.

Examples for C/5c – overcoming specific difficulties

Teachers overcome specific difficulties for individuals presented by aspects of the programmes of study and attainment targets through:

- using approaches to enable hearing impaired pupils to learn about sound in science and music
- helping visually impaired pupils to learn about light in science, to access maps and visual resources in geography and to evaluate different products in design and technology and images in art and design
- providing opportunities for pupils to develop strength in depth where they cannot meet the particular requirements of a subject, such as the visual requirements in art and design and the singing requirements in music
- discounting these aspects in appropriate individual cases when required to make a judgement against level descriptions.

Pupils who are learning English as an additional language

6 Pupils for whom English is an additional language have diverse needs in terms of support necessary in English language learning. Planning should take account of such factors as the pupil's age, length of time in this country, previous educational experience and skills in other languages. Careful monitoring of each pupil's progress in the acquisition of English language skills and of subject knowledge and understanding will be necessary to confirm that no learning difficulties are present.

7 The ability of pupils for whom English is an additional language to take part in the National Curriculum may be ahead of their communication skills in English. Teachers should plan learning opportunities to help pupils develop their English and should aim to provide the support pupils need to take part in all subject areas.

8 Teachers should take specific action to help pupils who are learning English as an additional language by:

a developing their spoken and written English

b ensuring access to the curriculum and to assessment.

Examples for C/8a – developing spoken and written English

Teachers develop pupils' spoken and written English through:

- ensuring that vocabulary work covers both the technical and everyday meaning of key words, metaphors and idioms
- explaining clearly how speaking and writing in English are structured to achieve different purposes, across a range of subjects
- providing a variety of reading material [for example, pupils' own work, the media, ICT, literature, reference books] that highlight the different ways English is used, especially those that help pupils to understand society and culture
- ensuring that there are effective opportunities for talk and that talk is used to support writing in all subjects
- where appropriate, encouraging pupils to transfer their knowledge, skills and understanding of one language to another, pointing out similarities and differences between languages
- building on pupils' experiences of language at home and in the wider community, so that their developing uses of English and other languages support one another.

Examples for C/8b – ensuring access

Teachers make sure pupils have access to the curriculum and to assessment through:

- using accessible texts and materials that suit pupils' ages and levels of learning
- providing support by using ICT or video or audio materials, dictionaries and translators, readers and amanuenses
- using home or first language, where appropriate.

Additional information for modern foreign languages

Teachers may find the following additional information helpful when implementing the statutory inclusion statement: **Providing effective learning opportunities for all pupils.** Teachers need to consider the full requirements of the inclusion statement when planning for individuals or groups of pupils.

To overcome any potential barriers to learning in modern foreign languages, some pupils may require:

- support in learning to understand, read and write a modern foreign language, including the use of ICT, particularly when they are unable to express themselves orally
- alternative communication systems, such as signing or symbols, to develop language skills and understanding
- help in learning to distinguish between the sounds of a particular language to compensate for difficulties in hearing
- support to compensate for difficulties in seeing visual cues or gestures when developing conversational language.

In assessment:

- pupils who are unable to communicate orally may be unable to complete the requirements of the attainment target relating to speaking. Pupils with hearing impairment may be unable to complete the requirements of the attainment target relating to listening and responding. When judgements against level descriptions are required, assessment of progress should discount these aspects of work.

Use of language across the curriculum

1 Pupils should be taught in all subjects to express themselves correctly and appropriately and to read accurately and with understanding. Since standard English, spoken and written, is the predominant language in which knowledge and skills are taught and learned, pupils should be taught to recognise and use standard English.[1]

Writing

2 In writing, pupils should be taught to use correct spelling and punctuation and follow grammatical conventions. They should also be taught to organise their writing in logical and coherent forms.

Speaking

3 In speaking, pupils should be taught to use language precisely and cogently.

Listening

4 Pupils should be taught to listen to others, and to respond and build on their ideas and views constructively.

Reading

5 In reading, pupils should be taught strategies to help them read with understanding, to locate and use information, to follow a process or argument and summarise, and to synthesise and adapt what they learn from their reading.

6 Pupils should be taught the technical and specialist vocabulary of subjects and how to use and spell these words. They should also be taught to use the patterns of language vital to understanding and expression in different subjects. These include the construction of sentences, paragraphs and texts that are often used in a subject [for example, language to express causality, chronology, logic, exploration, hypothesis, comparison, and how to ask questions and develop arguments]

[1] This does not apply to MFL but is included as the skills should be taught in the target language. Links to the English programme of study are indicated alongside the programme of study for MFL.

Use of information and communication technology across the curriculum

1 Pupils should be given opportunities[1] to apply and develop their ICT capability through the use of ICT tools to support their learning in all subjects (with the exception of physical education at key stages 1 and 2).

2 Pupils should be given opportunities to support their work by being taught to:
- a find things out from a variety of sources, selecting and synthesising the information to meet their needs and developing an ability to question its accuracy, bias and plausibility
- b develop their ideas using ICT tools to amend and refine their work and enhance its quality and accuracy
- c exchange and share information, both directly and through electronic media
- d review, modify and evaluate their work, reflecting critically on its quality, as it progresses.

[1] At key stage 1, there are no statutory requirements to teach the use of ICT in the programmes of study for the non-core foundation subjects. Teachers should use their judgement to decide where it is appropriate to teach the use of ICT across these subjects at key stage 1. At other key stages, there are statutory requirements to use ICT in all subjects, except physical education.

Guidelines

Guidelines for modern foreign languages at key stage 2

The contribution of modern foreign languages to the primary school curriculum

The learning of a foreign language in primary school provides a valuable educational, social and cultural experience for all pupils. Pupils develop communication and literacy skills that lay the foundation for future language learning. They develop linguistic competence, extend their knowledge of how language works and explore differences and similarities between the foreign language and English. Learning another language raises awareness of the multilingual and multi-cultural world and introduces an international dimension to pupils' learning, giving them an insight into their own culture and those of others. The learning of a foreign language provides a medium for cross-curricular links and for the reinforcement of knowledge, skills and understanding developed in other subjects.

Considerations

When planning to introduce a modern foreign language, schools need to consider:

- the aims and objectives for teaching a modern foreign language
- the choice of modern foreign language
- the age at which the language is to be introduced
- the availability of suitably trained teachers
- the amount and frequency of teaching time, including the number of weeks taught in the school year
- continuity and progression from class to class and from primary to secondary school.

The following are non-statutory guidelines

Key stage 2

There is no statutory requirement to teach a modern foreign language at key stages 1 and 2. The following guidelines are non-statutory and aimed at those primary schools that are teaching or planning to teach a modern foreign language.

The guidelines are designed for use with pupils in years 5 and 6. They may be adapted for use with other year groups in primary schools.

Knowledge, skills and understanding

While much of the programme of study for modern foreign languages at key stages 3 and 4 can be applied in primary schools, the following aspects are particularly relevant and have been suitably adapted.

Understanding and using the foreign language

1 In the early stages of language learning pupils might be taught:
- a how to use and respond to the foreign language
- b how to listen carefully in order to discriminate sounds, identify meaning and develop auditory awareness
- c correct pronunciation and intonation
- d how to ask and answer questions
- e techniques for memorising words, phrases and short extracts
- f how to use context and clues to interpret meaning
- g how to make use of their knowledge of English or another language in learning the foreign language.

2 Pupils can be taught about other countries and cultures by:
- a working with authentic materials including some from ICT-based sources
- b considering their own culture and comparing it with others
- c considering the experiences of other people.

3 In order to develop their knowledge, skills and understanding further, pupils might also be taught:
- a the interrelationship of sounds and writing
- b simple aspects of grammar and how to apply them
- c how to initiate conversations
- d how to use dictionaries and other reference materials
- e how to communicate with each other in the foreign language in pairs and groups and with their teacher
- f how to use their knowledge of the language creatively and imaginatively
- g how to use the foreign language for real purposes.

Links with other subjects

Learning another language presents opportunities for the reinforcement of knowledge, skills and understanding developed in other curriculum areas. These opportunities can be exploited through:

- aspects of English such as speaking and listening skills, knowledge and understanding of grammatical structures and sentence construction
- aspects of mathematics such as counting, calculations, money, the time and the date

- songs, alphabet, poems, rhymes and stories in other languages
- international or multi-cultural work, for example celebration of festivals, storytelling
- using ICT, for example e-mail with schools abroad, materials from the internet and satellite television
- geographical and historical work relating to other countries.

Attainment targets

The four attainment targets for modern foreign languages at key stages 3 and 4 can be applied as appropriate at key stage 2. They are:

- attainment target 1: Listening and responding
- attainment target 2: Speaking
- attainment target 3: Reading and responding
- attainment target 4: Writing.

Level descriptions

The following level descriptions are included to inform planning and to help evaluate pupils' progress. They may also be used when transferring information on pupils' competence from class to class and from one school to another.

Attainment target 1: listening and responding

Level 1

Pupils show that they understand simple classroom commands, short statements and questions. They understand speech spoken clearly, face-to-face or from a good-quality recording, with no background noise or interference. They may need a lot of help, such as repetition and gesture.

Level 2

Pupils show that they understand a range of familiar statements and questions [for example, everyday classroom language and instructions for setting tasks]. They respond to a clear model of standard language, but may need items to be repeated.

Level 3

Pupils show that they understand short passages made up of familiar language that is spoken at near normal speed without interference. These passages include instructions, messages and dialogues. Pupils identify and note main points and personal responses [for example, likes, dislikes and feelings], but may need short sections to be repeated.

Level 4

Pupils show that they understand longer passages, made up of familiar language in simple sentences, that are spoken at near normal speed with little interference. They identify and note main points and some details, but may need some items to be repeated.

Attainment target 2: speaking

Level 1

Pupils respond briefly, with single words or short phrases, to what they see and hear. Their pronunciation may be approximate, and they may need considerable support from a spoken model and from visual cues.

Level 2

Pupils give short, simple responses to what they see and hear. They name and describe people, places and objects. They use set phrases [for example, to ask for help and permission]. Their pronunciation may still be approximate and the delivery hesitant, but their meaning is clear.

Level 3

Pupils take part in brief prepared tasks of at least two or three exchanges, using visual or other cues to help them initiate and respond. They use short phrases to express personal responses [for example, likes, dislikes and feelings]. Although they use mainly memorised language, they occasionally substitute items of vocabulary to vary questions or statements.

Level 4

Pupils take part in simple structured conversations of at least three or four exchanges, supported by visual or other cues. They are beginning to use their knowledge of grammar to adapt and substitute single words and phrases. Their pronunciation is generally accurate and they show some consistency in their intonation.

Attainment target 3: reading and responding

Level 1

Pupils show that they understand single words presented in clear script in a familiar context. They may need visual cues.

Level 2

Pupils show that they understand short phrases presented in a familiar context. They match sound to print by reading aloud single familiar words and phrases. They use books or glossaries to find out the meanings of new words.

Level 3

Pupils show that they understand short texts and dialogues, made up of familiar language, printed in books or word-processed. They identify and note main points and personal responses [for example, likes, dislikes and feelings]. They are beginning to read independently, selecting simple texts and using a bilingual dictionary or glossary to look up new words.

Level 4

Pupils show that they understand short stories and factual texts, printed or clearly handwritten. They identify and note main points and some details. When reading on their own, as well as using a bilingual dictionary or glossary, they are beginning to use context to work out what unfamiliar words mean.

Attainment target 4: writing

Level 1

Pupils copy single familiar words correctly. They label items and select appropriate words to complete short phrases or sentences.

Level 2

Pupils copy familiar short phrases correctly. They write or word-process items [for example, simple signs and instructions] and set phrases used regularly in class. When they write familiar words from memory their spelling may be approximate.

Level 3

Pupils write two or three short sentences on familiar topics, using aids [for example, textbooks, wallcharts and their own written work]. They express personal responses [for example, likes, dislikes and feelings]. They write short phrases from memory and their spelling is readily understandable.

Level 4

Pupils write individual paragraphs of about three or four simple sentences, drawing largely on memorised language. They are beginning to use their knowledge of grammar to adapt and substitute individual words and set phrases. They are beginning to use dictionaries or glossaries to check words they have learnt.

The attainment targets for modern foreign languages

About the attainment targets

An attainment target sets out the 'knowledge, skills and understanding that pupils of different abilities and maturities are expected to have by the end of each key stage'[1]. Except in the case of citizenship[2], attainment targets consist of eight level descriptions of increasing difficulty, plus a description for exceptional performance above level 8. Each level description describes the types and range of performance that pupils working at that level should characteristically demonstrate.

The level descriptions provide the basis for making judgements about pupils' performance at the end of key stage 3. At key stage 4, national qualifications are the main means of assessing attainment in modern foreign languages.

Range of levels within which the great majority of pupils are expected to work		Expected attainment for the majority of pupils at the end of the key stage	
Key stage 3	**3–7**	at age 14	**5/6**[3]

Assessing attainment at the end of a key stage

In deciding on a pupil's level of attainment at the end of a key stage, teachers should judge which description best fits the pupil's performance. When doing so, each description should be considered alongside descriptions for adjacent levels.

Arrangements for statutory assessment at the end of each key stage are set out in detail in QCA's annual booklets about assessment and reporting arrangements.

Examples in the level descriptions

The examples in grey type are not statutory.

[1] As defined by the Education Act 1996, section 353a.
[2] In citizenship, expected performance for the majority of pupils at the end of key stages 3 and 4 is set out in end of key stage descriptions.
[3] Including modern foreign languages.

Attainment target 1: listening and responding

Level 1

Pupils show that they understand simple classroom commands, short statements and questions. They understand speech spoken clearly, face-to-face or from a good-quality recording, with no background noise or interference. They may need a lot of help, such as repetition and gesture.

Level 2

Pupils show that they understand a range of familiar statements and questions [for example, everyday classroom language and instructions for setting tasks]. They respond to a clear model of standard language, but may need items to be repeated.

Level 3

Pupils show that they understand short passages made up of familiar language that is spoken at near normal speed without interference. These passages include instructions, messages and dialogues. Pupils identify and note main points and personal responses [for example, likes, dislikes and feelings], but may need short sections to be repeated.

Level 4

Pupils show that they understand longer passages, made up of familiar language in simple sentences, that are spoken at near normal speed with little interference. They identify and note main points and some details, but may need some items to be repeated.

Level 5

Pupils show that they understand extracts of spoken language made up of familiar material from several topics, including present and past or future events. They cope with language spoken at near normal speed in everyday circumstances that has little or no interference or hesitancy. They identify and note main points and specific details, including opinions, and may need some repetition.

Level 6

Pupils show that they understand short narratives and extracts of spoken language, which cover various past, present and future events and include familiar language in unfamiliar contexts. They cope with language spoken at normal speed and with some interference and hesitancy. They identify and note main points and specific details, including points of view, and need little repetition.

Level 7

Pupils show that they understand a range of material that contains some complex sentences and unfamiliar language. They understand language spoken at normal speed, including brief news items and non-factual material taken from radio or television, and need little repetition.

Level 8

Pupils show that they understand different types of spoken material from a range of sources [for example, news items, interviews, documentaries, films and plays]. When listening to familiar and less familiar material they draw inferences, recognise attitudes and emotions, and need little repetition.

Exceptional performance

Pupils show that they understand a wide range of factual and imaginative speech, some of which expresses different points of view, issues and concerns. They summarise in detail, report, and explain extracts, orally and in writing. They develop their independent listening by selecting from and responding to recorded sources according to their interests.

Attainment target 2: speaking

Level 1

Pupils respond briefly, with single words or short phrases, to what they see and hear. Their pronunciation may be approximate, and they may need considerable support from a spoken model and from visual cues.

Level 2

Pupils give short, simple responses to what they see and hear. They name and describe people, places and objects. They use set phrases [for example, to ask for help and permission]. Their pronunciation may still be approximate and the delivery hesitant, but their meaning is clear.

Level 3

Pupils take part in brief prepared tasks of at least two or three exchanges, using visual or other cues to help them initiate and respond. They use short phrases to express personal responses [for example, likes, dislikes and feelings]. Although they use mainly memorised language, they occasionally substitute items of vocabulary to vary questions or statements.

Level 4

Pupils take part in simple structured conversations of at least three or four exchanges, supported by visual or other cues. They are beginning to use their knowledge of grammar to adapt and substitute single words and phrases. Their pronunciation is generally accurate and they show some consistency in their intonation.

Level 5

Pupils take part in short conversations, seeking and conveying information and opinions in simple terms. They refer to recent experiences or future plans, as well as everyday activities and interests. Although there may be some mistakes, pupils make themselves understood with little or no difficulty.

Level 6

Pupils take part in conversations that include past, present and future actions and events. They apply their knowledge of grammar in new contexts. They use the target language to meet most of their routine needs for information and explanations. Although they may be hesitant at times, pupils make themselves understood with little or no difficulty.

Level 7

Pupils initiate and develop conversations and discuss matters of personal or topical interest. They improvise and paraphrase. Their pronunciation and intonation are good, and their language is usually accurate.

Level 8

Pupils give and justify opinions and discuss facts, ideas and experiences. They use a range of vocabulary, structures and time references. They adapt language to deal with unprepared situations. They speak confidently with good pronunciation and intonation, and their language is largely accurate with few mistakes of any significance.

Exceptional performance

Pupils discuss a wide range of factual and imaginative topics, giving and seeking personal views and opinions in informal and formal situations. They deal confidently with unpredictable elements in conversations, or with people who are unfamiliar. They speak fluently, with consistently accurate pronunciation, and can vary intonation. They give clear messages and make few errors.

Attainment target 3: reading and responding

Level 1

Pupils show that they understand single words presented in clear script in a familiar context. They may need visual cues.

Level 2

Pupils show that they understand short phrases presented in a familiar context. They match sound to print by reading aloud single familiar words and phrases. They use books or glossaries to find out the meanings of new words.

Level 3

Pupils show that they understand short texts and dialogues, made up of familiar language, printed in books or word processed. They identify and note main points and personal responses [for example, likes, dislikes and feelings]. They are beginning to read independently, selecting simple texts and using a bilingual dictionary or glossary to look up new words.

Level 4

Pupils show that they understand short stories and factual texts, printed or clearly handwritten. They identify and note main points and some details. When reading on their own, as well as using a bilingual dictionary or glossary, they are beginning to use context to work out what unfamiliar words mean.

Level 5

Pupils show that they understand a range of written material, including texts covering present and past or future events. They identify and note main points and specific details, including opinions. Their independent reading includes authentic materials [for example, information leaflets, newspaper extracts, letters, databases]. They are generally confident in reading aloud, and in using reference materials.

Level 6

Pupils show that they understand a variety of texts that cover past, present and future events and include familiar language in unfamiliar contexts. They identify and note main points and specific details, including points of view. They scan written material, for stories or articles of interest, and choose books or texts to read on their own, at their own level. They are more confident in using context and their knowledge of grammar to work out the meaning of language they do not know.

Level 7

Pupils show that they understand a range of material, imaginative and factual, that includes some complex sentences and unfamiliar language. They use new vocabulary and structures found in their reading to respond in speech or in writing. They use reference materials when these are helpful.

Level 8

Pupils show that they understand a wide variety of types of written material. When reading for personal interest and for information, they consult a range of reference sources where appropriate. They cope readily with unfamiliar topics involving more complex language, and recognise attitudes and emotions.

Exceptional performance

Pupils show that they understand a wide range of factual and imaginative texts, some of which express different points of view, issues and concerns, and which include official and formal material. They summarise in detail, report, and explain extracts, orally and in writing. They develop their independent reading by choosing stories, articles, books and plays according to their interests, and responding to them.

Attainment target 4: writing

Level 1

Pupils copy single familiar words correctly. They label items and select appropriate words to complete short phrases or sentences.

Level 2

Pupils copy familiar short phrases correctly. They write or word process items [for example, simple signs and instructions] and set phrases used regularly in class. When they write familiar words from memory their spelling may be approximate.

Level 3

Pupils write two or three short sentences on familiar topics, using aids [for example, textbooks, wallcharts and their own written work]. They express personal responses, [for example, likes, dislikes and feelings] They write short phrases from memory and their spelling is readily understandable.

Level 4

Pupils write individual paragraphs of about three or four simple sentences, drawing largely on memorised language. They are beginning to use their knowledge of grammar to adapt and substitute individual words and set phrases. They are beginning to use dictionaries or glossaries to check words they have learnt.

Level 5

Pupils produce short pieces of writing, in simple sentences, that seek and convey information and opinions. They refer to recent experiences or future plans, as well as to everyday activities. Although there may be some mistakes, the meaning can be understood with little or no difficulty. They use dictionaries or glossaries to check words they have learnt and to look up unknown words.

Level 6

Pupils write in paragraphs, using simple descriptive language, and refer to past, present and future actions and events. They apply grammar in new contexts. Although there may be a few mistakes, the meaning is usually clear.

Level 7

Pupils produce pieces of writing of varying lengths on real and imaginary subjects, using an appropriate register. They link sentences and paragraphs, structure ideas and adapt previously learnt language for their own purposes. They edit and redraft their work, using reference sources to improve their accuracy, precision and variety of expression. Although there may be occasional mistakes, the meaning is clear.

Level 8

Pupils express and justify ideas, opinions or personal points of view, and seek the views of others. They develop the content of what they have read, seen or heard. Their spelling and grammar are generally accurate, and the style is appropriate to the content. They use reference materials to extend their range of language and improve their accuracy.

Exceptional performance

Pupils write coherently and accurately about a wide range of factual and imaginative topics. They choose the appropriate form of writing for a particular task, and use resources to help them vary the style and scope of their writing.

Modifications

Modifications for pupils studying Chinese (Cantonese or Mandarin) or Japanese

Chinese (Cantonese or Mandarin)

The level descriptions for **listening and responding** assume that Chinese may be spoken at a slower speed than indicated and that the range of topics may be more limited.

The level descriptions for **reading and responding** and **writing** assume that, as well as using pinyin, pupils can work with an approximate number of characters as indicated below. These should mainly be simple and frequently occurring characters that are relevant to the contexts for learning. It is expected that pupils can understand compound phrases and four character phrases (idioms).

	Reading and responding	Writing
Level 1:	20–30 characters	10–20 characters
Level 2:	30–60 characters	20–30 characters
Level 3:	60–100 characters	30–50 characters
Level 4:	100–150 characters	50–100 characters
Level 5:	150–250 characters	100–150 characters
Level 6:	250–350 characters	150–250 characters
Level 7:	350–450 characters	250–350 characters
Level 8:	450–600 characters	350–500 characters
Exceptional performance:	600 or more characters	500 or more characters

The level descriptions for **reading and responding** assume that characters that are beyond the level of pupils' development but appear in authentic materials may be glossed using pinyin or a similar romanised transcription.

Japanese

The level descriptions for levels 1 to 4 for **reading and responding** and **writing** assume that pupils' script capability has developed so that they can work with the following:

Level 1: hiragana symbols
Level 2: hiragana symbols and modifications [for example, nigori]
Level 3: hiragana and katakana symbols and modifications
Level 4: hiragana, katakana and 20–40 kanji

The level descriptions for level 5 and above for **reading and responding** and **writing** assume that, as well as using hiragana and katakana and any modifications, pupils can work with an approximate number of kanji as indicated below. These should mainly be simple and frequently occurring kanji that are relevant to the contexts for learning.

	Reading and responding	Writing
Level 5:	40–90 kanji	40–60 kanji
Level 6:	90–140 kanji	60–90 kanji
Level 7:	140–200 kanji	90–140 kanji
Level 8:	200–270 kanji	140–220 kanji
Exceptional performance:	270 or more kanji	220 or more kanji

The level descriptions for **reading and responding** assume that kanji that are beyond the level of pupils' development but appear in authentic materials may be glossed using kana.

Acknowledgements

About the work used in this document
The artwork and photographs used in this book are the result of a national selection organised by QCA and the Design Council. We would like to thank all 3,108 pupils who took part and especially the following pupils and schools whose work has been used throughout the National Curriculum.

Pupils Frankie Allen, Sarah Anderson, Naomi Ball, Kristina Battleday, Ashley Boyle, Martin Broom, Katie Brown, Alex Bryant, Tania Burnett, Elizabeth Burrows, Caitie Calloway, Kavandeep Chahal, Donna Clarke, Leah Cliffe, Megan Coombs, Andrew Cornford, Samantha Davidoff, Jodie Evans, Holly Fowler, Rachel Fort, Christopher Fort, Hannah Foster, Ruth Fry, Nicholas Furlonge, Tasleem Ghanchi, Rebecca Goodwin, Megan Goodwin, Joanna Gray, Alisha Grazette, Emma Habbeshon, Zoe Hall, Kay Hampshire, Jessica Harris, Aimee Howard, Amy Hurst, Katherine Hymers, Safwan Ismael, Tamaszina Jacobs-Abiola, Tomi Johnson, Richard Jones, Bruno Jones, Thomas Kelleher, Sophie Lambert, Gareth Lloyd, Ope Majekodunmi, Sophie Manchester, Alex Massie, Amy McNair, Dale Meachen, Katherine Mills, Rebecca Moore, Andrew Morgan, Amber Murrell, Sally O'Connor, Rosie O'Reilly, Antonia Pain, Daniel Pamment, Jennie Plant, Christopher Prest, Megan Ramsay, Alice Ross, David Rowles, Amy Sandford, Zeba Saudagar, Nathan Scarfe, Daniel Scully, Bilal Shakoor, Sandeep Sharma, Morrad Siyahla, Daryl Smith, Catriona Statham, Scott Taylor, Amy Thornton, Jessica Tidmarsh, Alix Tinkler, Lucy Titford, Marion Tulloch, Charlotte Ward, Kaltuun Warsame, Emily Webb, Bradley West, Daniel Wilkinson, Soriah Williams, Susan Williamson, Helen Williamson, Charlotte Windmill, Ryan Wollan, Olivia Wright.

Schools Adam's Grammar School, Almondbury Junior School, Bishops Castle Community College, Bolton Brow Junior and Infant School, Boxford C of E Voluntary Controlled Primary School, Bugbrooke School, Cantell School, Charnwood Primary School, Cheselbourne County First School, Chester Catholic High School, Dales Infant School, Deanery C of E High School, Driffield C of E Infants' School, Dursley Primary School, Fourfields County Primary School, Furze Infants School, Gosforth High School, Grahame Park Junior School, Green Park Combined School, Gusford Community Primary School, Hartshill School, Headington School, Holyport Manor School, Jersey College for Girls Preparatory School, King Edward VI School, King James's School, Kingsway Junior School, Knutsford High School, Leiston Primary School, Maltby Manor Infant School, Mullion Comprehensive School, North Marston C of E First School, Norton Hill School, Penglais School, Priory Secondary School, Redknock School, Richard Whittington Primary School, Ringwood School, Sarah Bonnell School, Sedgemoor Manor Infants School, Selly Park Technology College for Girls, Southwark Infant School, St Albans High School for Girls, St Denys C of E Infant School, St Helen's C of E (Aided) Primary School, St John's Infants School, St Joseph's RC Infant School, St Laurence School, St Mary Magdalene School, St Matthews C of E Aided Primary School, St Michael's C of E School, St Saviour's and St Olave's School, St Thomas The Martyr C of E Primary School, Sawtry Community College, The Duchess's High School, Tideway School, Torfield School, Trinity C of E Primary School, Upper Poppelton School, Walton High School.

QCA and the Design Council would also like to thank the figures from public life who contributed their ideas about the value of each curriculum subject.